After the Wedding

After the Wedding

A Postnuptial
Recipe for
Creating a
Healthy, Happy
Marriage

Jack H. Grossman, Ph.D.

TABLE OF CONTENTS

Acknowledgements ....*vii*

Preface ....*ix*

Introduction...xi

Now That the Ceremony Is Over 1

What Is Marriage – Really? 5

What, Specifically, You Can Look Forward to As Partners 11

A Reminder of What You Promised Each Other................19

The Power of Love 31

A Brief Review 43

    Reminders of Our Actual and Implied Promises...............45

    Essentials for Keeping Our Marriage Flame Aglow 47

    Behaviors and Attitudes That Demonstrate Trustworthiness.........48

ACKNOWLEDGEMENTS

I owe a special thanks to these people:

My son, Gary, who always insists that my writings and the ways they are presented meet his extraordinary standards. Your editorial assistance, Gary, has added greatly to the quality of this book.

My old friend, Larry Hammond, who added his editorial skills to sharpen the presentation. Your critical eye has made a significant difference in the final version of this volume.

My new friend, Pete Danis, who encouraged me to add a spiritual dimension to this book. That dimension, which was missing in my first draft, adds a quality that makes this book richer. To quote Pete, "The recognition of God's hand in our married lives is a critical ingredient in helping us with the many trials and tribulations married people experience."

All four of our children — Lynn, Gayle, Michael, and Gary — taught us that, to be good parents, Joan and I had to be kind and respectful to each other. So, out of regard to our children, as well as to each other, we became committed to making our marriage work. Thank you for helping us to fulfill our marital vows.

My wife, Joan, who, in addition to being my best friend for the length of our marriage, taught me to be the husband I am today, and, with the aid of our children, taught me to be the father I have enjoyed being. No words can fully express my sincere feelings for your genuine love.

After the Wedding was inspired in part by three questions I invariably asked myself whenever we attended a wedding. Those questions were:

- When people exchange marriage vows and the bride and groom agree to honor their promises to each other by saying, "I do," are they aware of what they actually are promising?
- Are they aware of what it takes to fulfill those promises?
- When couples say, "I love you" to each other, both before and after their wedding, what besides the words are they really saying?

After the Wedding is my attempt to answer those questions. It contains thoughts to ponder and discuss, as well as activities that will help both of you to achieve your reasonable expectations and desires. You will also learn how to talk respectfully with each other and how to resolve your differences civilly. In short, when used properly, *After the Wedding* can strengthen your marriage and improve your individual lives.

Although there is no special time to read this book, consider doing so during stressful times and on your anniversaries.

By the way, I invite you to contact me via my e-mail (jack@grossmanpartners.com) to let me know how useful my recipe has been for creating a healthy, happy marriage. If you would like to share additional ingredients that have worked for you, you are invited to do so.

Best wishes,

Jack

JACK H. GROSSMAN

In 1977, I wrote a series of short essays to my wife, Joan, about the nature of love as I understood and felt it. Abbey Press published them as an illustrated book under the title, *The Promise of Love*. The themes of these essays were based on my 15 years experience as a marriage therapist and my 21 years of marriage.

As a marriage counselor, I frequently heard both men and women complain about the non-loving, insensitive treatment their respective spouses exhibited toward each other. When members of the couples were made aware of the pain they inadvertently caused their respective partners, many couldn't believe it. "Why would I want to hurt someone I love?" they asked, not really expecting an answer. Of course they wouldn't deliberately cause each other pain. Is it possible, however, that they really didn't understand the true meaning of love?

I believe Joan and I understood intuitively, from the moment we exchanged our vows, how married couples are supposed to act toward each other. But intuition was not enough. Since we were committed to making our marriage work, we made a conscious effort to fulfill our commitment. Furthermore, we rarely allowed negative influences to deter us from honoring our marriage vows.

During our 47 years of marriage, we learned about love from the joys and sorrows we experienced together, from the numerous pleasures we shared and from the many adversities we overcame. Our love also deepened and strengthened as we successfully met the challenges of rearing four children who blessed us with seven grandchildren. What, you may ask, has been our secret? We diligently practiced the principles we discovered through trials and errors – principles discussed in this book.

In addition, as I reflect on our life together, I realize we were not alone. We had spiritual guidance that enabled us to practice the common sense principles we discovered — principles that have proven to be effective and that obviously have stood the test of time. In essence, I realize that God provided us with gifts that helped us enjoy our life together and that enabled us to solve problems and resolve our differences. The gifts we were blessed with constitute our core beliefs and shared values, as well as the strength and patience to create a loving family and a sacred relationship that works.

CHAPTER ONE

Now That the Ceremony Is Over

Reasons for getting married vary. Some are emotional and others are rational. Still others are both emotional and rational. Regardless of your reasons, ultimately the foundation of a lasting, healthy marriage is a genuine loving relationship.

As you'll discover with time, the cornerstones of love are mutual respect and trust. The ability to understand and demonstrate these two qualities takes practice. Practice involves rational, conscious activity. Furthermore, it takes practice to be sincerely respectful and trustworthy during good times and bad. The good news is that practice over time is part of a growth process that will help make your new relationship richer, stronger and more fun than you ever thought possible. Such practice will also make your love last.

Staying happily married for as long as you promised when you took your vows takes dedication and considerable effort. In addition to managing challenges and opportunities you faced individually before your marriage, you must now consider the feelings and desires of each other when making important decisions. That added consideration obviously increases the number and complexity of your challenges.

This is not meant to scare you. Rather, it is meant to heighten your awareness of the investments you must make if you are to enrich your life and enjoy the opportunities your marital relationship can offer. My point is that marriage can be a relationship where one plus one equals more than two, but it requires commitments from both of you. Each of you has to do your part to make the relationship work and prosper.

Realize this: If two people want to continue liking each other and having fun together, they both have to act like responsible adults. Marriage is not for children, regardless of how old they are. To succeed, it takes two mature people who can talk civilly with each other, who are willing to work out their differences when they arise and who want to help each other be better human beings.

That's a tall order. Yet, judging from all the happily married couples I have known, it can be done. In the time we have together, I will explain how, and show you what you can do, to build a solid marital foundation that can serve you through all phases of your life. Despite changes that occur during the course of your marriage, you still can achieve marital bliss if your foundation is strong and if both of you consistently work at strengthening and building on that foundation. Through the activities contained in this book, you will also learn, should your marital spark dim, how to rekindle your relationship and transform it into a healthy, happy marriage.

Let's start at the beginning.

CHAPTER TWO

What Is Marriage—Really?

Regardless of the actual reasons you had for making your life-long partnership holy and legal, this event is a milestone worthy of recognition and attention. It's a milestone because a good marriage provides new opportunities for a level of partnership, commitment and enlightenment that did not exist before your union.

To help you view your marriage as a milestone, realize it takes work for marriage to work. Often during courtship when couples are in love they temporarily are blind to each other's weaknesses, as well as to the realities of married life. But it doesn't take long for them to regain 20/20 vision. When they do, the process of building a healthy marriage actually begins.

The amount of time it takes to overcome love-induced blindness differs for each couple. Eventually, however, all couples realize it takes more than physical attraction to keep their marriage alive with excitement. You probably realized this fact already. Chances are, you already discovered that you have to extend yourself to make your relationship with your spouse vibrant and special. Regardless of your knowledge and education, you can never learn too much about how to strengthen a relationship as complex and special as marriage.

I know what many people say. They say that after the honeymoon the magnetism that originally attracts two people to each other weakens. They say that couples can't expect their feelings toward each other to last, or to be as strong as they were during their courtship. But it doesn't have to be that way. Don't you know, just as I do, many married couples whose love strengthens with time? How do they do it, you ask? How do they hold on to and build on the powerful loving emotions that prompted them to say, "I do" on their wedding day? They do it by consistently honoring their vows to each other and by not losing sight of what it means to be a loving and caring person.

Before we go further, I want you to keep a thought in mind. It's my simple definition of love. You won't find this definition in the dictionary. But, when you think about it, you will agree that it makes sense. You will also agree that genuine love is the foundation for everything else we'll be discussing. Here is the definition:

LOVE IS
MUTUAL RESPECT AND TRUST
SPICED WITH
ALL THE SPECIAL FEELINGS
THAT ATTRACT TWO PEOPLE
TO EACH OTHER.

Without mutual respect and trust, the spice that once attracted a loving couple to each other eventually loses its potency. When that happens, their love withers and finally dies. With mutual respect and trust, spice gives love the power and zest a couple needs to face life's challenges and to enjoy their life together.

Do you agree? Assuming you said yes, let's continue with my recipe for building on the special feelings and powerful emotions that prompted the two of you to say, "I do" on the day you were pronounced husband and wife.

The basic ingredients of this recipe are kind and loving attitudes you must consistently exhibit toward each other and toward your marriage. Because these attitudes are vital to building a happy, long-lasting partnership, you need to see them in action. Make a point some time of observing happily married people you know. Listen to them talk to each other; watch how they treat one another. They are so tender and considerate. It's as if each views the other as the most important person in their lives.

You can also see these attitudes expressed by two harmonious and successful business partners. Maybe marriage is not exactly like a compatible business partnership, but they are not that much different. Think about it for a moment. Why would two people form a business partnership? One big reason is that both parties have abilities and other attributes that complement each other's. Or, maybe each lacks qualities or skills their partner-to-be possesses. It doesn't matter who needs what. The important thing is that both believe that together they would be better off than each could be alone.

You see, it would not make any sense for them to become partners if they had the same temperament, abilities, interests, skills, and other personal qualities. But when two people believe they can add value to each other, and are convinced that they can help each other prosper, the thought of becoming partners is appealing.

Building a healthy, happy marriage is no different. You, being an equal partner, must believe you are a lovable, respectable, and an important person in your own right, worthy of a partner with similar merits. You also must believe that by uniting with another person who is just as loveable, respectable, and important as you, you can each make a better life for yourselves than you could if you traveled life's journey solo. Don't you agree that building on this belief is a pretty good way of approaching this serious relationship? I know it sounds a bit idealistic, but it certainly is an ideal worth shooting for. Why? Because, when you reach that ideal, one plus one actually does become more than two.

Maybe as newlyweds you don't think of yourself and your mate as partners. But it's never too late to structure your relationship so it becomes a healthy, compatible partnership – one in which you benefit from each other's strengths and offset each other's weaknesses. It's worth a try. Once you decide to do that, you will enjoy a relationship that will bloom like beautiful flowers in a fertile garden.

One attitude that encompasses all loving attitudes – an attitude that may be viewed as the mother of all loving attitudes -- is a variation of the Golden Rule. It is:

TREAT YOUR SPOUSE AS HE OR SHE WOULD LIKE TO BE TREATED

We will employ this aphorism as the basis of an exercise I will ask you to do later. In the meantime, let's consider what you can gain by creating a healthy, happy, loving partnership.

CHAPTER THREE

What, Specifically, You Can Look Forward to As Partners

The first benefit you can look forward to when you become loving partners is that problems you will face or situations you'll encounter are yours to work out together. How do you like that for a comforting prospect?

Another benefit you can enjoy by having a mate who is a genuine and compassionate partner is that you can be yourself, as long as being yourself is not destructive to your partner. It's a good feeling to disrobe emotionally and to let your hair down with someone you care for, respect, and trust, and who also cares deeply for you. Sure, I suppose you can do a little of that with your other friends. But you and I know that they have their own problems. Although they care about you, your friends are not the same as a loving partner. Your loving partner makes time for you when you need it and is emotionally committed to helping you resolve problems that might arise.

If those benefits aren't enough, consider the good times you can have with a loving marital partner. It's not that difficult to imagine. Just think about why you liked each other's company before you married; also think about all the things you enjoyed doing together. Why should those enjoyable activities stop because you married? The fact is, you can still have fun together and share the joys of living. I'm sure you would agree that it's even more fun to do things with someone you view as a special friend than with an ordinary friend.

Being soul mates is another benefit. Happily married couples I know who enjoy all the pleasures of a loving relationship consider each other soul mates and, therefore, have a genuine interest in each other's well being. They also are greatly affected by each other's emotions – both negative and positive. When one of the partners is in a bad mood or is not feeling well, it upsets the other, and the relationship temporarily suffers. But when good fortune visits either partner, there is nobody with whom they would rather share their good feelings, or with whom they would rather celebrate the occasion, than with each other. Because they are soul mates, both partners do everything in their power to be each other's **best** friend.

I'm sure you know what makes two people be each other's best friend and how they behave toward each other. Since the characteristics of such a friendship are vital to its health, they are worthy of special notice.

Best friends listen to each other – really listen – without passing judgment. They help lift their friend's spirit when he or she is "down." They extend themselves to and for each other, i.e. they offer help when it's needed. And, of course, they don't purposely say or do anything that is hurtful. Even when they disagree, they try not to be disagreeable. This last characteristic is so important that it's worth repeating: When best friends disagree, they try not to be disagreeable. As you would expect, all those right actions strengthen their relationship. You can be sure of that.

But being a concerned and devoted partner, a best friend, exacts a price. It's a small price, but a price nevertheless. Each of you has to accept qualities about your partner that you may not like or understand. "So," you might ask, "why would my spouse put up with them?" You might also ask, "Why should I put up with my spouse's craziness?" The answer to both questions is the same. Each of you must believe your partner's many good qualities overshadow those you have difficulties accepting because you do not understand them, or because you consider them offensive. For those reasons, you have to focus on the good qualities and learn more about, or learn to accept, those qualities that are not appealing to you.

One of the positive images that comes to mind when I get upset with Joan dates back to the day I was scheduled to take my oral exam, which was the last hurdle before I could receive my doctorate diploma. It is a three-hour ordeal with three professors directing questions at the doctoral candidate.

The questions could deal with anything we had studied over the years leading to this moment. What made this event important was that students who failed this exam had to wait a year before they could retake it.

Joan, knowing how nervous I was and how much I studied for the exam, took off her wedding band and gave it to me just before I was ready to depart. I'll never forget her words: "Although I can't be with you physically, I want you to know I am with you in spirit. When things get rough squeeze the ring; it will help you get through the pain."

It did. That gesture followed by her warm embrace and kiss gave me the confidence I needed to perform well.

She employed other loving gestures over the years; gestures that said, "Although you are going through a tough time, I am with you emotionally, spiritually and mentally. Remember, you are not alone."

I think of those love-motivated gestures whenever I get angry with Joan. As you might predict, those thoughts help me resolve my anger quickly.

Believing their partner's good qualities overshadow the not-so-good ones is one of the loving attitudes happily married couples adopt.

Is each of you willing to adopt this attitude? I hope you are. Why? Because **couples who are not**

happily married do just the opposite: they take for granted their spouse's good qualities, and make a big deal out of the not-so-good ones.

Don't take your spouse's good qualities for granted. Find effective ways of letting go of your anger when it is triggered. One way of doing that is to think of a wonderful quality that makes your spouse really likeable, if not loveable. Hold on to that thought until your anger passes. Another way is described below.

Early in our marriage I would get annoyed at Joan's short fuse and her temper when things were not going as well for her as she would have liked. When I got annoyed I also lost my temper, which exacerbated her emotional state. The result was that both of us became angry at each other. Well, I must tell you, this was not good for either of us.

After a year or so of this nonsense, I found a way of dealing with Joan's temperament. I viewed her anger simply as a storm passing. Just as I couldn't get rid of a storm by yelling or by getting angry at it, I could not effectively deal with Joan's anger by getting upset with her. All that did was fuel the fire. By viewing it as a passing storm, I knew that time will take care of it if I exercised patience and said nothing while the "storm" ran its course. My strategy worked much of the time. In fact, saying nothing when negative emotions are intense has been a good strategy for me in many situations.

Joan found her own ways of dealing with my behaviors that angered her. One of my favorites is her offer to make something for dinner that is particularly appealing to me. Or, she offers to make and join me in a cup of coffee.

Her strategy has worked very well. After all, how could I remain angry with someone who is so pleasant toward me? In fact, this strategy worked so well that I have employed variations of it myself.

To repeat, don't take your spouse's good qualities for granted. When you get angry, find your own creative ways of letting go of your anger so you can move forward with your lives.

All the attitudes happily married couples possess demonstrate that they take seriously and honor both the *implied* and *actual* promises they made when they exchanged their marriage vows. Let's next consider the implied promises **_you_** made to each other.

CHAPTER FOUR

A Reminder of What You Promised Each Other

The first, and most important, implied promise you made is to get to know each other's inner world – your likes and dislikes, your needs and desires, your vulnerabilities, your values, and whatever other qualities define each of you as the person you are. Learning what each of you wants from life and needs from each other will increase your respective sensitivities so both of you can respond lovingly to each other's unique and complex world.

TIME OUT

Take a break for as long as you need to before you embark on the following exercise.

Effective communication is a bridge that connects two disparate worlds. In this first exercise, which I call, "Getting to Know You," you will take a major step toward strengthening the bridge that currently connects the two of you. All the subsequent exercises collectively will (when done conscientiously) reinforce the bridge so that, while you successfully manage the challenges and opportunities life has to offer, you also grow together as stronger partners.

EXERCISE 1

.

Getting to Know You

Preparation for Your Discussion

Separately, complete in writing the following two statements to reflect your true feelings:

1. I'd appreciate it if you would _____.
   Describe all your specific and reasonable expectations, i.e. reasonable entitlements. Then, on a scale of 1 (low) to 10 (high) rate the degree to which each expectation is fulfilled.

2. It sure would be nice if you would _____.
   Describe those things you desire from your spouse. Desires refer to actions you wish your spouse would occasionally exhibit to make you feel extra special. That is, although you don't expect those behaviors, it sure would be nice if he or she exhibited them. Then, as with the expecta-

tions, rate the degree to which these desires are actually fulfilled.

Discussing Your Lists

Starting with your respective lists of expectations, alternately discuss each one. That is, Person One reads the first statement and its rating. Discuss it until you are both pleased with the result of your discussion. Next, Person Two reads his or her first statement, which is then discussed until an agreement is reached. Continue this until both your lists are fully discussed. Next, do the same thing with your respective "wish lists", i.e. your desires. *Remember, since you don't expect wishes, the degree to which they are fulfilled is considerably lower than expectations. But that's O.K.*

Tips on How to Make These Discussions Productive

Don't argue with your partner's expectations. The key here is that these should be discussed, but not defended. If for some reason you consider a particular one unreasonable and cannot fulfill it, a productive discussion can result in a valuable compromise. Invest the time to make this discussion productive and not defensive. This opportunity can clear up many misunderstandings.

If you can fulfill an expectation to a higher degree than you have in the past, promise your partner that you will make a sincere effort to do so. Make sure your spouse is convinced of your sincerity by explaining how things will be different.

Do not, under any circumstances, undermine or make your spouse feel guilty for expressing any expectation or desire.

I urge you to do this exercise from time-to-time, either partially or fully, to keep the lines of communication open. Why? Because it's so easy, when two people become busy with their daily activities, to forget about each other's needs. You can't let that happen or you'll drift apart. By having these discussions you'll discover changes in each other and learn how you can realistically adjust to them.

Joan works, as do I, but she also cooks dinner because she prefers to do that over going to a restaurant. However (I suspect you knew this was coming), she expects me to set the table, clear the table after we eat and load the dishwasher.

Early in our marriage I did not volunteer for the aforementioned "domestic role." But when we had one of our discussions, I agreed that this expectation was reasonable. So I gladly took over this function much of the time. We both have felt good about this arrangement, which of course is flexible, as are all our agreements.

Another discussion, quite recently, revolved around our social life. One day Joan said, "I'm getting tired of being responsible for coming up with entertainment ideas." Her complaint was quite legitimate because for the most part I don't care what we do or where we go. So, I rely on her and, with her permission, dubbed her our Social Chairman. Well, she wanted to relinquish that job. But I wasn't willing to assume that function completely. After some discussion we agreed to split the job. So far it has worked out to both our satisfactions.

A second *implied* promise you made when you took your marriage vows is to be forthright and sensitively honest with each other. Holding grudges or playing the children's game, "I know something you don't know and I bet you can't guess what it is," rather than expressing your feelings openly, is destructive to your relationship. So is keeping negative feelings bottled up inside you and using them to build tall, thick walls that are impossible to get through or around.

You must have the courage to express what's bothering you. However, you must do it in ways that will not damage your partner. Being sensitive to your spouse's feelings is not easy. Realize, however, that what you say as well as when and how you express your feelings makes a huge difference. So, instead of expending energy being nervous about how your spouse will react, you can invest thought in your delivery. Strategic delivery of a message requires some forethought as well as trial and error, but success yields great rewards.

Another of your *implied* promises was not to remake each other into your image of the person you believe your partner ought to be. Sounds like a mouthful. But think about it this way: When you took your vows you said, "I do." You did not say, "I do, on the following conditions: _____." Rather, you accepted each other for whom and what your partner-to-be was, not what you would like him or her to be, or not what you believed you can make him or her become.

But that doesn't mean you shouldn't encourage and help each other to develop valuable qualities that are lying dormant within each of you. In fact, it's a good idea to provide such encouragement. Why? Because when each of you expands your interests, skills, and experiences and shares them with each other, both of you will grow. That's how one plus one becomes more than two. **When that happens you really have a profitable partnership!**

A fourth *implied* promise you made is to not take each other for granted. This, as I am sure you realize, is a vital promise because when it is broken you are saying, in effect, "I don't have to think about how I talk to you or treat you, since you're mine and I no longer have to impress you. I no longer have to be sensitive to your needs." Of course, that isn't what you want to communicate. Yet, that's the message you convey when you take your spouse for granted.

People who take each other for granted believe that all the benefits they receive from their partner are coming to them, regardless of their behaviors. Well, you and I know that's simply not true. In fact, this attitude is the single biggest cause of marital conflicts and breakups. To convince yourself of that statement, reflect for a moment on couples that have had difficulties keeping their marriage alive and vibrant, or even together. Don't one or both parties take each other for granted? Aren't their behaviors toward each other less than respectful? You know the answer to that question as well as I do.

You can fulfill some of your implied promise of not taking each other for granted by honoring simple courtesies and civil behaviors, many of which we learned as children and adolescents, while others we learned as adults. Consider these for starters:

- Say "please" and "thank you." Being polite does not cost anything and it always is appreciated.

- Call if you're going to be late or if you have to break an appointment. Everyone's time is valuable.
- Talk nice and ask, don't demand. This is the old adage, "You get better results with honey than with vinegar."
- Express appropriate appreciation when your partner extends him or herself for you. He or she chose to do it and, if you encourage your spouse, he or she may choose to do it again.
- Avoid activities and/or discussions that might embarrass your spouse in public.
- Don't undermine your spouse in private. Genuinely apologize if you've said or done something you know, or have been told, is inappropriate.
- Don't ignore each other. Demonstrate spontaneous and periodic appreciation for having your partner in your life.
- Be considerate of and kind to each other. You have a lot invested in each other; take care of that investment so it can take care of you.

REMEMBER:

TREAT YOUR SPOUSE
AS HE OR SHE WOULD
LIKE TO BE TREATED

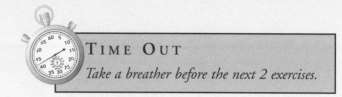

TIME OUT

Take a breather before the next 2 exercises.

EXERCISE 2
•
How We Will Be Respectful Toward Each Other

Just as you did with the first time out, begin this exercise independently. Separately, think of actions you can exhibit that will demonstrate your implied promise to be respectful toward your spouse, i.e. not to take your marital partner for granted. Write them down so they will serve as a reminder to you. Call them your I will ____ (or I promise to ____) list and I won't ____ (or I promise not to ____) list.

When you've completed compiling these two lists, share and alternately discuss each item with your spouse, similar to the way you did in the previous exercise. Your objective here is to ensure each other that you will exhibit mutual respect, which is the opposite of taking each other for granted.

Mutual trust, as you know, is the other cornerstone of a loving relationship. To fulfill your marriage commitments, you must agree on how you will demonstrate trust toward each other.

Before you embark on the next exercise, consider the following three general attitudes concerning mutual trust:

- I would not do anything to purposely hurt or disappoint you.
- I would not misuse information or feelings you share with me.
- I would not say or do anything that might cause you to be afraid of me. After all, how can you trust me to be a genuine and loving partner if you're afraid of me?

With those guidelines, proceed to the following exercise.

EXERCISE 3
·

How We Will Be Trustworthy Toward Each Other

It stands to reason that each of you is more likely to trust your spouse if your spouse is worthy of trust.

(See: *Behaviors and Attitudes That Demonstrate Trustworthiness* in the Review section of this book.) Now, let's move on with the exercise.

Independently, complete this sentence: **I can trust you fully if** _____. Separately, think of actions your spouse can exhibit or avoid that will demonstrate his or her implied promise to be trustworthy. E.g. when I share my feelings about a situation, don't belittle them.

When you've completed your lists, share and alternately discuss each item with each other, similar to the way you did earlier.

YOUR OBJECTIVE IN THIS
EXERCISE IS TO IMPROVE YOUR
MUTUAL TRUST.

So much for your implied promises. There is one additional promise, however, that you did not <u>imply</u>. It was an actual promise. It was the promise to love each other. Do you remember? Because it was a real promise, I will give it special consideration and talk about the power and the true meaning of the words, **"I love you."** I'll also talk about what loving couples can do to prevent their relationship from becoming stale.

CHAPTER FIVE

The Power of Love

The Power of Love,
What "I love you" Really Means
and
How to Prevent Your Marriage From Becoming Stale

As a refresher, let's revisit my definition of love.

LOVE IS
MUTUAL RESPECT AND TRUST
SPICED WITH
ALL THE SPECIAL FEELINGS
THAT ATTRACT TWO PEOPLE
TO EACH OTHER.

Love has extraordinary power when respect and trust between two people are spiced with strong positive emotions. Married couples can exercise that power to make each other feel either good or bad. They, more than anyone else, can affect each other's emotional being.

Are you aware of the extent of your power? It is enormous. A loving word or gesture from either of you can probably charge your spouse with an enthusiasm for living and a will to excel. That's good. But it's also true that your rejection, lack of understanding, or your insensitive comments, can hurt your partner deeply and make him or her less effective as a person. That's obviously not good, nor kind or loving. *Think about this paragraph and discuss it.*

Knowing how much power you have over your partner is like having a loaded weapon. In the heat of discussions or misunderstandings that might arise, appreciation for its power combined with a genuine love for your partner can help you use it like Cupid's arrow instead of like an enemy's gun.

A good start to learning how to use your power effectively is to actually promise each other that you will never *intentionally* misuse it. That promise should include an agreement that if it is misused the "offended party" has permission to remind the "offending party" of the promise. As long as the reminder is delivered and received with love and respect, this can be a productive walk along your communication bridge. This walk will not only prevent destruction of the bridge, it will reinforce the love, respect and trust that created it.

Now let's talk about all the possible meanings of, "*I love you.*" You've probably said it often to each other. When you are sincere, those three words speak volumes. They say such things as:

- "I care for you deeply. I am willing to share myself with you, emotionally, spiritually, intellectually and physically without fear or reservation."
- "You are important to me. I value everything about you. This includes all of your unique *human* qualities."
- "You make me feel wanted and needed in a way no one else can. You make me feel that I am a very special person in your eyes."
- "I feel a warmth and selflessness that encourages me to be generous with my time and attention."
- "I think about you even when you are not with me. I think of ways to brighten your day and to make you feel good."

Are those *your* sentiments when you say, "I love you" to your spouse? Perhaps you have other feelings you would like to share with each other.

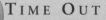

TIME OUT

Take a breather before the next exercise.

Exercise 4

·

What "I love you" Means to Me

Both of you may have additional thoughts and feelings when you say, "I love you" to each other. What are those thoughts and feelings? How about taking a few minutes, or as much time as you'd like, to write your responses (note the plural) to this partial sentence: **When I say, "I love you" I feel or think** _____. Don't hold back. This can be a prelude to an exciting evening (or afternoon). Next, take turns, one item at a time, reading to each other what you wrote.

Your personal thoughts and feelings, as well as those I described, are both rational and romantic ways of personalizing and giving life to those three magical words – I love you.

Talking about magic, if you want to experience that feeling for the life of your marriage, you must commit yourself to being co-creators of that magic. There is no trick to working the magic; nor does it require a sleight of hand. "So," you ask, "how can we accomplish this feat?" Assuming you are sincere, you must jog your memory as you go through the following process:

Remember all those **fun** things you did together during your courtship? Do you remember the **spon-**

taneous things you did together? They weren't always rational. But you didn't care because that's what loving people do – they laugh and have fun together. They are playful with each other – like children. Can you think of any reason why you can't maintain that spontaneous quality in your relationship? All it takes is some imagination on both your parts.

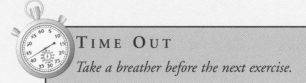

TIME OUT
Take a breather before the next exercise.

EXERCISE 5
•
Planned Spontaneity

Put time aside to do this fun exercise as a couple. I call it, "Planned Spontaneity." Think of some spontaneous things you can and would like to do together and write them down (you need to make only one list). Make the list as long as ideas come to you, and be creative. Put the list away for future reference, making sure to add to it when the spirit moves you. When the time is right (only you can determine when that is), consult your list, agree on an activity you would like to do, and just do it.

Here is another idea you can each initiate alone. Surprise your spouse with something you know he or she would appreciate (Remember the "It sure would be nice if _____" list?) Doesn't that sound like a fun thing to do? And, imagine how surprised your spouse will be.

The point is that your marriage can never become stale if you think of creative ways to revitalize and recharge your relationship regularly. All that's required to keep you on a healthy track are the following three attitudes:

We can make our marriage as good as we want it to be because we control our marital destiny.

•

It's up to us as partners to decide what we want our marriage to be like.

•

It's up to us to decide how we can achieve what we want – individually and together.

If each of you honors your commitments to your partnership and to each other, think of the possibilities you can realize.

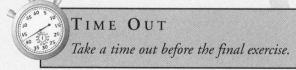

TIME OUT
Take a time out before the final exercise.

In this final exercise, you will see how each of you views your relationship as it currently exists. You will then discuss your respective views and talk about what each of you must do to achieve the kind of partnership both of you desire. Some of the issues you'll discuss will be similar to those covered in earlier exercises. But that's O.K, as long as the discussion moves you to your objective, which is characterized by the title of this exercise.

EXERCISE 6
·
Determine the State of Your Current Relationship *and* How You Can Achieve a Genuine Partnership

What follows is a pictorial description of a healthy and ideal partnership. It depicts two equal sized overlapping circles representing a man and woman. Notice that each person maintains his and her individuality, but they also contribute to their common bond that consists of shared values, interests, and any other characteristics that hold their relationship together. Their desire to contribute to the bond and their willingness to learn from each other make this a strong, growing relationship.

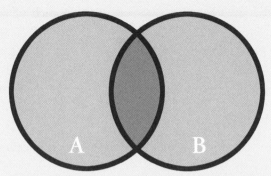

A Pictorial Description of a Healthy and Ideal Partnership

What follows are pictorial descriptions of not-so-healthy marital relationships. These depict three couples whose relationships fall short, to different degrees, of the ideal. In the first one (**I**) the couple seems to have no common bond that binds them. In effect, they lead independent lives and function like roommates. In relationship two (**II**), "B" is totally engulfed by "A." It's as if "B" has no life of his or her own and is completely dependent on "A." Furthermore, judging from their difference in size, "A" is superior to "B." The third relationship (**III**) is better than the second, but not that much. "B" still needs to develop more of a life for him or herself.

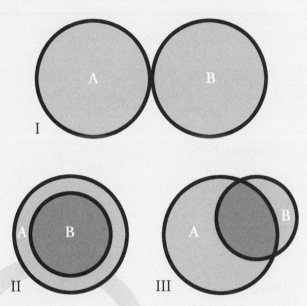

Pictorial Descriptions of Not-So-Healthy Marital Relationships

Your Task

On separate sheets of paper, and without consulting each other, pictorially describe your **current** marital relationship. (*Realize that the nature of your relationship is not permanent, which makes the exercise you are about to do interesting and even exciting.*) After completing your drawings, follow the instructions below.

Compare your individual pictorial descriptions of your relationship with each other. If you described your relationship differently, **discuss** each of your reasons for seeing it as you do. Don't argue about your different perceptions; just present them with your reasons. You can see things differently, but that doesn't mean one of you is wrong and the other is right. Do you agree? Now is also a good time to discuss or re-discuss your mutual expectations and desires.

Important Note: To prevent arguments during this exercise, honor the following two communication principles:

- Do not make statements that begin with a "you," and are followed by a negative comment or generalization, such as "you don't," "you aren't," "you never," or "you always."
- Do not make any comments that place your partner on the defensive, such as, "Why didn't you _____?" "How many times have I told you _____?" "If you didn't _____." Well, I'm sure you get the idea.

Next, compare both your pictorial descriptions to the ideal and discuss the differences. Talk about specific implied promises each of you needs to fulfill to make your relationship healthier and happier. Talk about what each of you can do specifically to:

- Strengthen the bonds that can keep you together.
- Strengthen the communication bridge that can improve your connection.

In short, discuss what each of you can do to get closer to the ideal relationship.

Best Wishes for a Healthy, Happy Marriage.

From someone who cares: J.H.G.

APPENDIX

A Brief Review

Weeks, sometimes months, after I have read a useful informational book, I like to go back and review some of the author's key points. So, I look for the material I highlighted. While that is somewhat satisfying, I often wished the author had summarized those key points in an Appendix. Assuming you have had similar thoughts, I decided to include this review and urge you to refer to it as often as you need to.

This review includes the following summaries:

Reminders of Our Actual and Implied Promises to Each Other

•

Essentials for Keeping Our Marriage Flame Aglow

•

Behaviors and Attitudes That Demonstrate Trustworthiness

Reminders of Our Actual and Implied Promises to Each Other

- I promise to get to know you as a person – emotionally and intellectually – including your qualities that I understand as well as those I just accept. I also promise to be aware of what you want from life and need from me.

- I promise to be forthright and honest, rather than hold grudges. This will help us build productive bridges rather than invisible, insurmountable walls.

- I promise to be trustworthy in my attitudes and actions. (What that means specifically is presented separately under the title, *Behaviors and Attitudes That Demonstrate Trustworthiness*.)

- I promise to accept and respect your unique qualities. Therefore, I promise not to remake you into my image of the person I believe you ought to be.

- I promise to focus on your strengths and help to offset or better understand how to accept your weaknesses.

- I promise to contribute all I can to your personal growth and to the growth of our partnership so that all three of us (you, me and our marriage) prosper emotionally and intellectually.

- I promise not to take you for granted, ever. (What that means specifically is presented separately under the title, *Essentials for Keeping Our Marriage Flame Aglow.*)

- I promise to do everything in my power to maintain my love for you and to always be in-love with you.

Essentials for Keeping Our Marriage Flame Aglow

KEY PRINCIPLE:
Never, Ever Take Each Other for Granted

How to honor this principle:

LISTEN to each other's emotions, as well as words.

RESPECT each other's reasonable needs and wants.

RESPECT each other's differences.

RESOLVE problems before parting for the day or going to sleep.

AVOID being defensive and placing each other on the defensive.

BE CONSIDERATE of each other's feelings and be kind to each other.

GIVE each other the benefit of our doubts.

TAKE TIME to make each other feel special.

BE CORDIAL toward each other. Remember "please" and "thank you."

In short, treat each other as we would like to be treated —as a cherished friend and lover.

Behaviors and Attitudes That Demonstrate Trustworthiness

Marital partners need to depend on and confide in each other. They need to share feelings and thoughts that cannot be divulged to anyone else. Without mutual trust these needs cannot be fulfilled. The degree of trust your spouse will have in you is directly related to your own trustworthiness.

REMEMBER:
TO BE TRUSTED,
EACH OF YOU MUST BE
CONSISTENTLY TRUSTWORTHY.

The behaviors and attitudes described below reflect some specific ways of achieving that objective. You will find it useful to discuss them.

- Do not say or do anything to deliberately hurt your spouse.
- Do not use anything your spouse has said or done as a destructive weapon. For example, don't ever say, "I told you so."
- Do not make your spouse regret or feel guilty for bringing up a problem that involves you.
- Be truthful and open about things that matter to both of you. Do not build invisible walls between you.

- Be available emotionally, if not physically, when your spouse needs you; do not undermine your spouse's emotions by saying such things as, "You shouldn't feel that way" or "You're overly sensitive."
- Follow through on your promises to fulfill your partner's requests.
- Do not make promises you cannot fulfill.
- Resist the temptation to be jealous of any attention or recognition your spouse receives from others.
- Maintain your spouse's confidence.
- Consistently be considerate of your spouse.